Question Text	Topic	Option 1	Option 2	Option 3	Option 4	Correct Option

How to write cache function or equivalent in Python? Which of the following Code can help in the same	Introduction to Python	def collatz(n):
		  sequence = []
		  sequenceLength = 0
		  while (n>=1):
		    if n in sequence:
		      break
		    else:
			sequenceLength = 0
			while (n>=1):
			  if n in sequence:
			    break
			  else:
				sequence.append(n)
				if (n==1):
				  break #
				solution is found
				elif (n%2==0):
				  n = n/2
					solution is found
					elif (n%2==0):
					  n = n/2
					sequenceLength += 1
						1

Please select all the options that are executable statements in Python?	Introductin to Python	Class	Def	Import	All of the above	4
QuerySet now is <QuertSet[<value: 5>, <value:90>]> How I can get 5, 90 to separate variable ? Which command in Python can help in this?	Introductin to Python	Query List	Value list	Definition List	Plan List	2

Question	Topic	Option 1	Option 2	Option 3	Option 4	Answer
What is the command in python to print a string which contains "Output: "	Introductin to Python	Leng/	OP/	IO?	Print(' \" ')	4
Which is the right Python code for Parallel Vectors? Please select the right option?	Introductin to Python	def isOrthogonal(self,v ,tolerance=1e-10): if abs(self.dotProduc t(v)) < tolerance: return True return False	def isOrthogonal(self,v ,tolerance=1e-10): if	abs(self.dotProduct (v)) < tolerance:	v)) < tolerance: return True return False	1
using listingspackage to put a python code inside an article. We want it to be written in \ttfamily. The problem is that we can't change keywordstyle to bold text? Which command can solve this issue?	Introductin to Python	Keystroke Option	Imodern with the lighttt option	Dark Option	None of the above	2
What is the maximum no of arguments that help function can take? Please select the below options?	Data Handling in Python	one	Two	three	Four	1

Question	Category	Option 1	Option 2	Option 3	Option 4	Answer
If you don't need to cast the Command spell to tell the snake what do, do you spend an action to do so? Which command can be given?	Data Handling in Python	Normal Command	Sub normal Command	Mental Command	Spell Command	3
Which of the methods can solve How to solve this differential equation numerically in Python?	Data Handling in Python	Implicit Method	Euler Method	Both of the above	None of the above	3
We are trying to solve the back substitution in Python? import numpy as np A = np.matrix([[1,1,-1],[0,1,3],[0,0,-6]]) b = np.array([9,3,8]) def back_sub(A,b): n = len(A)	Data Handling in Python	print(b[i]) b[i] = b[i] - A[i,j]*x[j] print(i,A[i,j],x[j]) print(b[i]) print('--')	print(i,A[i,j],x[j])	print(b[i])	print('--')	1
Is there a way to store a function in a list or dictionary so that when the index (or key) is called it fires off the stored function? like mydict = {'funcList1': [foo(),bar(),goo()], 'funcList2': [foo(),goo(),bar()], which doesn't work. Which commander can help in the same?	Data Handling in Python	Dispatcher-foobar	dispatcher = {'foobar': [foo, bar], 'bazcat': [baz, cat]}	None of the above	Dispatcher-baz,cat	2

Question	Category	Option 1	Option 2	Option 3	Option 4	Answer
How to extract data from namedtuple in file handling in python? Which command can help?	Data Handling in Python	Print?S	print("%s\t%d\t%s \n" % line)	Print?Line	None of the above	2
How do we merge a value and a range or list in python in a single line? We would like to combine 1 and range(3) to get a list [1,0,1,2]. Select the righ option?	Data Cleaning and Treatment	>>> import numpy as np >>> np.r_[1,0:3] array([1, 0, 1, 2])	>>> np.r_[1,0:3]	array([1, 0, 1, 2])	None of the above	1
What are the techniques to Handling Incoming Data from Multiple Sockets in Python	Data Cleaning and Treatment	Asynchronous Library-Twisted	Asynchronous Library-G Event	Asynchronous Library-Tornado	All of the above	4
Which is the command below can help how to handle a small grid of data in Python?	Data Cleaning and Treatment	Namedtuple	Non tuple	None of the above	Grid Tuple	1

What are the ways to Handle large data pools in python? Select the best options?	Data Cleaning and Treatment	Pytables	Scipy	Numpy	All of the above	1
What are the commands and methods for the Proper way to handle variable data types in Python	Data Cleaning and Treatment	None	Vector	Segment	All of the above	1
How to handle binary data in commoncrawl using python? Which command can help? Please select the right option	Data Cleaning and Treatment	Pytables	Python- Magic	Right Magic	Data Magic	2
How Do we Change the Data Stored in a Text File in Python? Which command can help do the same?	Data Cleaning and Treatment	Do not call Truncate	None of the above	we need to call data.truncate()	Call Text file	3

Question	Category	Option A	Option B	Option C	Option D	Answer
What is the fastest method for converting a binary data string to a numeric value in Python? Please select the functionality in Python from the below options?	Data Cleaning and Treatment	unst.pack from()	Stru.Unpack()	None of the above	struct.unpack_from(),	4
We are getting the following errorw when we are executing the code? data = pd.read_csv("S:/<File1.csv>" data.dtypes All of the columns are read in as object types except for the first and last columns. var1 - var7 are all categorical variables with many levels in the middle of the dataset: categorical_features = ['var1','var2','var3','var4','var5','var6','var7'] for col in categorical_features: #for each categorical col dummies = pd.get_dummies(data[col], prefix=col) #one-hot-encoding	Data Cleaning and Treatment	Correction in df['var1'].running	Checking the names of columns uploaded with the CSV fie	Replacing getitem with get dummies	All of the above	4
The dataset involved has a feature called 'TimeStamp' in the following format, Month12 Day9 10:20:00. There are over 100k of such entries. We want to change all of these in the following format 2013-07-04 00:00:00 strptime() to parse a string into a datetime object, and strftime() to format a datetime object into a string Which can help solve the issue?	Data Cleaning and Treatment	import re regex = r"Month(?P<month>\d{2}) Day(?P<day>\d{1,2}) (?P<time>\d{2}:\d{2}:\d{2})" result = r"2012-	Month(?P<month>\d{2}) Day(?P<day>\d{1,2}) (?P<time>\d{2}:\d{2}:\d{2})"	\g<month>-0\g<day> \g<time>" # Assuming the year is 2012	import re regex = r"Month(?P<month>\d{2}) Day(?P<day>\d{1,2}) (?P<time>\d{2}:\d{2}:\	1
We have some test data scraped and struggle in how to clean it correctly in terms of efficiency. test_data = ['\r\n \r\n ', '\r\n ', 'Reine Baumwolle', '\r\n ', '\r\n \r\n ', '\r\n ', 'Kontrastblende am Ausschnitt', '\r\n ',	Data Cleaning and Treatment	Subject Comprehension	List Comprehension	Data Comprehension	Issue Comprehension	2

We want to create a new column for the text data (every row for that column is one description) after removing all numbers (such as 189, 98001), special characters (' , _, ", (,)), and letters with numbers or special characters (e21x16, e267, e4, e88889, entry778, id2, n27th, pv3,). def standardize_text(df, text_field): df[text_field] = df[text_field].str.lower() df[text_field] = df[text_field].str.replace(r'(', '') df[text_field] = df[text_field].str.replace(r')', '') df[text_field] = df[text_field].str.replace(r',', '')	Data Cleaning and Treatment	Use - from textcleaner import	!pip install textcleaner	import textcleaner as tc	All of the above	4
All of our data is in CSV files, most of which have ~10 columns and < 2,000 rows. The cleaning involves removing some rows, adding a few others, and splitting them up into CSV files by column values (date, in this case). The output is usually a dozen CSV files of "clean" data. Which command can help in Python?	Data Cleaning and Treatment	CSVed	Cved	Dataed	Columned	1
What we are attempting to do is use a sub selection of rcid's to conditionally change another column. The text file has all the rcid values we want to change in it, and we want to apply it to va_yes column. When we tried this we get an error "NameError: name 'rcid' is not defined". we have tried this before with one decade , but want to have all of it cleaned in one go. import numpy as np import pandas as pd df = pd.read_csv("C:\Users\Adini\Documents\opec_pooled.csv")	Data Cleaning and Treatment	Df-isin*1	df['va_yes'] = df['rcid'].isin(mylist) * 1	Va=yes	struct.unpack_from(),	2
How to index a Series value and deal with duplicate values indices in Python? we got a database of customers'orders and have to clean the columns UserPhone. In this columns, a value can be a str (ie: 0909111111, 0909.111.111) or number (ie: 909111111, 909111111.0, 84909111111). We want the result to be: 909111111. Code import pandas as pd test=pd.read_excel('D:/relay-foods.xlsx')	Data Cleaning and Treatment	test['UserPhone'] = test['UserPhone']	stype(str).str.replace('\.0$|^0|^84	test['UserPhone'] = test['UserPhone'].astype(str).str.replace('\.0$|^0|^84|[^0-9]+','').astype	None of the above	3

Question	Category	Option A	Option B	Option C	Option D	Answer
We are graph analysis on a .csv file for performing analytics.We are trying delete the rows having null values in their column in python. Sample file: Unnamed: 0 2012 2011 2010 2009 2008 2005 0 United States of America 760739 752423 781844 812514 843683 862220 1 Brazil 732913 717185 715702 651879 649996 NaN 2 Germany 520005 513458 515853 519010 518499 494329 3 United Kingdom (England and Wales) 310544 336997 367055 399869 419273 541455 What are the approaches to finalize this -	Basic Statistics,Graphs, Reports in Python	cleaned_data = data.dropna(how='any')	Data=why?Clean	Unclean-data=data	None of the above	1
-- | MANDT|BUKRS|NETWR |UMSKS|UMSKZ|AUGDT |AUGBL|ZUONR | -- | 100 |1000 |23.321- | | | | |TEXT I WANT TO KEEP| | 100 |1000 |0.12 | | | | |TEXT I WANT TO KEEP| | 100 |1500 |90 | | | | |TEXT I WANT TO KEEP| -- Expected Outcome	Basic Statistics,Graphs, Reports in Python	using built-in str object functions:	using re.sub() function:	Both of the above	None of the above	3
What are the available libraries for creating pretty charts and graphs in a Python application?	Basic Statistics,Graphs, Reports in Python	Cairo Plot	Matplolib	Both of the above	None of the above	3
What commands can help in Creating undirected graphs in Python?	Basic Statistics,Graphs, Reports in Python	i Graph	Network X	Both of the above	None of the above	3

Question	Subject	Option 1	Option 2	Option 3	Option 4	Answer
What data structure will be fast but also memory efficient?	Basic Statistics,Graphs, Reports in Python	Dicts	Dicts*Dicts	Subject	None of the above	1
What is the right python code to plot the graph in python? Select from the below options?	Basic Statistics,Graphs, Reports in Python	import matplotlib.pyplot as plt x = [x_coordination] y = [y_coordination] plt.plot(x, y)	Seaborn: import seaborn as sb x = [x_coordination] y = [y_coordination] sb.pointplot(x, y)	plt.show()	All the above	4
What are the different types of graph generators in python?	Basic Statistics,Graphs, Reports in Python	Atlas	Classic	Expanders	All the above	4
For a library for gathering "runtime statistics" in python, by which we mean an interface for outputting structured log files? Which systems are the best suited?	Basic Statistics,Graphs, Reports in Python	Graphite	MMStats	Both of the above	None of the above	3

Question	Category					Ans
What are the below options - for a package that handles statistics in Python?	Basic Statistics,Graphs, Reports in Python	Numpy	Scipy	Both of the above	None of the above	3
We need to compute combinatorials (nCr) in Python but cannot find the function to do that in math, numpy or stat libraries.Which of teh following is the best option(s)?	Basic Statistics,Graphs, Reports in Python	scipy.misc.comb	comb.scipy	misc.scipy	None of the above	1
We need to superimpose two Voronoi plots in Python import numpy as np import scipy.spatial as sp import matplotlib.pyplot as plt points = np.array([[0, 0], [0, 1], [0, 2], [1, 0],[1,1],[1, 2], [2, 0], [2, 1],[2, 2]]) vor=sp.Voronoi(points) sp.voronoi_plot_2d(vor) point_bis=np.array([[0.5,0.5],[1,1.5],[1.5,1],[2,2.5]])	Basic Statistics,Graphs, Reports in Python	fig, ax = plt.subplots() points = np.array([[0, 0], [0, 1], [0, 2], [1, 0],[1,1],[1, 2], [2, 0], [2, 1],[2, 2]]) vor=sp.Voronoi(points)	import numpy as np import scipy.spatial as sp import matplotlib.pyplot as plt fig, ax = plt.subplots()	point_bis=np.array([[0.5,0.5],[1,1.5],[1.5,1],[2,2.5]]) vor2=sp.Voronoi(point_bis) sp.voronoi_plot_2d(vor2, ax=ax)	mport scipy.spatial as sp import matplotlib.pyplot as plt fig, ax = plt.subplots() points = np.array([[0, 0], [0, 1], [0, 2], [1, 0],[1,1],[1, 2], [2, 0], [2, 1],[2, 2]]) vor=sp.Voronoi(points) sp.voronoi_plot_2d(vor, ax=ax)	2
Which commands can help graph module dependencies in Python ? Select from the below options	Basic Statistics,Graphs, Reports in Python	hg clone --insecure <src> <dest>	Snakefood	Both of the above	None of the above	3

Question	Topic					Answer
Does class declaration statement cause memory allocation in python? Is this statement true or False? Please choose the correct option	Introduction to Python					TRUE
All keywords in python are in lowercase. State True or False	Introduction to Python					FALSE
In pyhton can Identifier be of any length ? State whether the statement is true or False?	Introduction to Python					TRUE
State whether no or yes - . Do you need to cast the Command spell to tell the snake what to do in python	Data Handling in Python					yes

State true or false - the below statement - Would it be possible to use a variable as a function name in python	Data Handling in Python					TRUE
An object can contain the references to other objects? State whether this is true or False	Data Handling in Python					TRUE
State whether the case is true or false - The objective is to scrapped off tables from pdf file. That has been done with the tabula package and we have a CSV file. Can we do without Without your scraping source code	Data Handling in Python					TRUE
Is creating a dynamic graph with timestamped edges always? - True or False	Basic Statistics,Graphs, Reports in Python					TRUE

For Notes Making

For Notes Making

For Notes Making

For Notes Making

For Notes Making

For Notes Making

For Notes Making

For Notes Making

For Notes Making

For Notes Making

For Notes Making

For Notes Making